THE TANTRAMAR RE-VISION

THE HUGH MacLENNAN POETRY SERIES
Editors: Allan Hepburn and Carolyn Smart

TITLES IN THE SERIES

The Tantramar Re-Vision

KEVIN IRIE

McGill-Queen's University Press

Montreal & Kingston • London • Chicago

ISBN 978-0-2280-0637-4 (paper)
ISBN 978-0-2280-0741-8 (ePDF)
ISBN 978-0-2280-0742-5 (ePUB)

Legal deposit third quarter 2021
Bibliothèque nationale du Québec

Printed in Canada on acid-free paper that is 100% ancient forest free
(100% post-consumer recycled), processed chlorine free

We acknowledge the support of the Canada Council for the Arts.

Nous remercions le Conseil des arts du Canada de son soutien.

Library and Archives Canada Cataloguing in Publication

Title: The Tantramar re-vision / Kevin Irie.

Names: Irie, Kevin, 1953– author.

Series: Hugh MacLennan poetry series.

Description: Series statement: The Hugh MacLennan poetry series |
   Poems.

Identifiers: Canadiana (print) 2021020446X | Canadiana
   (ebook) 20210204508 | ISBN 9780228006374 (paper) |
   ISBN 9780228007418 (ePDF) | ISBN 9780228007425 (ePUB)

Classification: LCC PS8567.R48 T36 2021 | DDC C811/.54—dc23

This book was typeset by Marquis Interscript in 9.5/13 Sabon.

CONTENTS

THE TANTRAMAR RE-VISION

And yes, I was alone;
how could I not be?

Louise Glück

I write what I can't

Resist.

Jericho Brown

RECOGNITION

Fog finds its shape in the bodies that breach it –
a cow, a leaning barn, a man
coming closer to just being seen.

You know him by the way he walks, stands,
and how it is not the fog that contains him

but the dark which holds him in place.

DEFEATED (A CONFESSION)

My daydreams defeat me
John Thompson

Haven't I moved through life
    like heat through dry grass,

unseen but everywhere,
    explosive as a spark

that may never catch fire,
    a reflection on water that never

gave its own light?
    I've lived the way a field is sometimes

a shelter for mice
    or sometimes a source of game

for a hawk, the way
    my past is a growing family

of different people I used to be
    with identical fingerprints

shared among strangers
    too embarrassed to admit

what they did as each other.
    I imagined myself as one above many

who lived the life I wanted
for mine, my shortcomings

like judgments held against them,
uncertain of whom I scorned the most:

those who saw through my lies
or trusted their source. I've lived like a leaf

blown through scrub and dirt,
knowing what isn't followed

needn't fear being caught,
so close to the ground

as if below notice,
carried so far away with my faults

I've left whoever I was
in the distance,

willing to give up on being believed
in order to become a story

others want to hear.
I've fallen like snow that

is rain finally tired of
being just tears, that ends the crying

by turning to ice.
The self that I'd toss away like a stick

is also the self that wants to fetch
　　and be petted when

attention is handed to me as a leash.
　　And how difficult is it

to let people see me as far
　　as I let them? As difficult as it is

to confess even this,
　　when I'm acting close

to being myself.
　　As hard as catching

a current pulled under
　　by the very water

it is.

THE TANTRAMAR RE-VISION

Follow the path like a rip to its edge,

     a scar down its seam,

follow the route,

          no road,
              just a trail

straight as a finger that points from no hand
past marshland farms and further fields
where wind has the place
     all to itself.

Feel the chill draw out that self you've hidden,
         the one who leaves
         so many
         cold.

Who cares if the sky's been breached
by bad weather? If the day can't even
settle itself?
         Out on the marsh,
wind is wired all day,
unable to stop
till dusk brings it down.

Snort that cold up your nostrils,
     feel the buzz hit your flesh –

a sting akin
            to a knife-slit palm

licked
        like a line of coke.

Fresh air feels like a tab on the tongue

            to give you a taste
            of what rushes through you –

you're the surge of a creek on a downhill run,

        the hours cleared of minutes,

            then time.

    Ahead: there's a pond clear as
a vein without blood, just pebbles and stones
to weigh it down,

                pebbles small
                as a shot-off toe,

                stones thrust deep
                into muddied pockets.

How distant from life each breath feels
when you can't even stand being near
            yourself –

        the future
        a place on hold for now –

                    a leap of the mind
too far for the body.

And who'd even come here but the odd lost stranger,
          far from what others wish you'd be –

the only place large enough to hold the loathing
              you can't quite bring yourself
                        to contain
inside you.

Dead buds shrivel to warts on stems, nipples
no one wants in their mouth

the way no one wants who you are
among others.

Alive in these moments
when you stay outside them,

you are not to be found in the person you are.

              When you raise your rifle,
              you don't hear silence.

              Your future
              recoils in your ears.

Bales of rolled hay large
        as industrial oil drums.
        Grasses pulled
        to one side of the wind.

All along the highway,
        the past keeps changing its boundaries,
        won't stay off your part
        of the road.

Empty barns collapse
        like a starving herd
        with nothing inside to keep them
        standing.

Fence posts tilt
        like aimed rifles.
        Volleys of white clouds disperse
        in the breeze.

You're driving to the new life you're hoping to lead,
        leaving behind several
        you hope
        won't follow.

Don't be fooled if the road looks clear for the moment.
        Your past
        is always
        ahead of you.

CAUTIONARY

Listen. Heard somewhere –
a trickle, a fall,
as water moves closer to
being its sound –
a creek,
        a stream,

  some word to contain it,

a splash pulled under
the surface it rose from,

        the way some push themselves
into a silence that
others can't enter

but know is there.

A hook is indifferent to what it can
kill. Trout, a blur

beneath the surface. Let out the reel.
A line to keep moving failure

along. Winch the water up through itself,
how even emptiness feels

its own weight. Pull in whatever
hope draws toward you. How easily

loss finds itself water. How pain
drags through a body

like a line through a pond. How a trout
draws out praise from the end

of a hook.

LURE

Curved feather,
red, orange, yellow,
a spray of threads as a firework fountain
tied to
one bite.

A spurt of red blood
spat from a cut. The flicked fire
of a cigarette
landing in water.

Small anchor that plummets but not to sink.

Crank baits, spinner baits,
the bento minnow –

the paints, the coatings,
the fluorescent tassels brilliant as stamens on

the wedge, the penetrator, the rogue, the bully –
how a hook needs to be served by its lure the way

a stem needs its crucial work
done behind foliage. Needs the kind of names

perfect to enter a ring
and take down competitors

like *king rage, mister twister, the blade.*
To land a sharp right to a trout's open jaw

then watch it try to stagger away.
Does a *molix lover* love

the act or the catch, plying
its plastic for a fair trade

in death? To seduce a victim
out of the weed bed with a lure's open eyes

ready to serve
no life it can see? How *tail dancer,*

skitter walk, and *chug bug* stare
blindly for hours in their assigned death watch,

not wanting to do it, yet not unwilling,
while we peer from the boat

like a despot leaning over the palace balcony,
hopeful that luck will be on board

with our plans.
That when the future arrives,

we're still behind it. Like pulling
small bones of a trout through your teeth to get

all the meat, bait wants to separate
whatever resists away from

the body it was born
to capture. A point to remember,

knowing fish eat worms,
relative to the kind that later eat us.

MARSH MAP LEGEND

Here is a list
                lengthened

by its liquid lineage –

King's Marsh,

          Great Marsh,

                    Ram Pasture.

Labels you know for the landscape you don't –

          East Coles Island,

                    Jolicure Marsh.

No name you give will take it all in –

          Lower Mill Creek Marsh,

                    Dixon Island.

Places where the marsh stays held within paper
spill out of the page,

                    sink underfoot

as trails disappear
          down paths they expose

and farms pull in what's left of dry land,

          each crop a worry
          ahead of its time

as grass fills the emptiness
                              and then

excludes it.

There's Bear Island Marsh,

          Westcock and Westmorland.

Sunken Island.

None of this visible from the distance of paper
where the compass rose steers its wheel
to a corner,

          spins off,

                              lost.

Everything in its place
                    but direction.

          Everything knowing its place

but the map.

You know the direction. It's the way
you aren't sure of. A view you didn't
expect to be seen lies bare before you,

courtesy of the Marsh Visitor Centre.
Its revamped wetlands made sight-specific:
the once deemed empty

now branded as filled. A raised boardwalk
ramps up the impression you're
closer to water though you're more

like a raccoon at a sunken koi pond
where edges precisely canted at angles
keep you from making

any direct contact in the way that
Narcissus failed to forestall.
Repetition is rendered

by reeds at the shoreline
where much looks equal but nothing
stands out, where too often

nothing means just what you can see.
Brown scum shed by waves
could be snakeskins moulted by the movement

of each undulation. Drifting twigs and leaves
mingle and merge past a beaver lodge
disabled by its own solidity

from joining the flow. Decay and debris
floating a crowd-sourced creation.
Ahead, signs point you away

from more scenery: *Do not enter. Stay on paved roads.*
But what makes sense may not make for perspective.
As if a woodland path can be pulled

from its forest. As if a trail is only
the dirt that defines it. Don't even joke about
the improved parking lot paved

with good intentions.
We justify what we can of ourselves.
Does the past have *any* place

all for its own? Apparently not.
Or maybe past here. Clearly a place where
you no more belong than

you're welcome to linger uninvited.
There's sumac and dogwood taking position
against random shrubs of mass profusion

whose constancy fails to unite as one form.
Then there's phragmite, hogweed, purple loosestrife.
At home in places

they should not be. According to signage,
those plants are invasive, a resiliency to be envied
or outright killed. *Proceed with caution,*

watch your step,
since advances don't preclude
a setback ahead. See that pool –

where there used to be cattails?
They've vanished completely. Reflect on that.
There's no off-season

when it comes to change.
This marsh keeps to corners you'll never reach,
knows not even Nature

can hold on to its looks.

A CREEK AS COMPLICITY,
DUPLICITY, DARING

Something moves downstream
   past thinking of us:

a creek,
   one of water's lesser ambitions,

treading just inches
   above the ground, a shallow creature

that will never have depth,
   just a trough for land that lowers

to drink it. As if missing
   a turn off, it wanders, lost,

but won't stop for directions –
   such a typical male,

without any gender,
   though who knows if identity

serves itself well?
   Nature has a way of showing its hand

is not human, or perhaps
   too much so,

as the creek flips a beetle onto its back
   then sends it downstream

with tiny limbs waving
   like windshield wipers

on a sinking vehicle pulled below.
   And a new feather

small as a lifted thumbprint
   is wiped down clean

as it floats on the current,
   a feather forfeited

under terms and conditions
   we'll never know

though its waterproof oils
   still function at full capacity,

despite its missing body parts.
   But when isn't death

a lasting commitment
   with some partner

less than fully engaged,
   like these physical fragments,

now animal, now mineral,
   orphaned to shapes that will never

be given specifics again?
   Is it true equanimity

or truer indifference
  when the pawned and polluted

are provided with transit
  to ride on the creek together

for free, like the fecal brown bubbles
  or floating dead husks

that swivel and spin atop the water
  as they trade positions

in a quick game of chance
  to guess what's under

each overturned cup?
  There's no way of knowing

the future's position or how much
  time it will give to ours,

but you can bet it's better prepared.
  It's the way that a creek,

no matter the hour,
  remains on call

to deal with any mess:
  the diarrhetic spread

of near-liquid algae, the water weeds
  frayed as torn-off duct tape,

stems thin as wristbands
   in soiled beds. It's how a creek flows

the way a lost man plummets,
   scraping itself

on the sides of the banks
   like someone whose fingers

can't find a grip –
   another life run to the ground.

CURRENT

The sludge-slow flow of the visible current
opens a path we can't continue, tugs
at what no hand can pull along.

It's how even water loses memory,
travels a direction it cannot find,
a vein cut loose of its own skin,
to separate itself from what it belongs to –
depth, surface,
flow,
source.

>   *Keep moving*,
it says, without a word

as it takes the plunge to free what was form
into no shape it knew
it could be.

There is an oxbow forming in
      a stagnant water
  filled
  with inaction,
a loose loop of ribbon about to be pulled
and knotted.
        Tied for good.

Having no route in or thought to get out,
it slows like an old mind coming down
    to a memory –
This is dry land; I've been safe here before –
      a glimpse
of how time flows back into itself the way
what's remembered
becomes what's occurred.

The curve of a trout caught on a hook
    after the thrashing
    stops.

WINDBLOWN

In
>   the marsh grass,

wind
>   stirs up some business

I don't know about.

>   It riffles
>   through leaves,
reeds,

discreetly withdraws

>   a small amount of seeds
to deposit elsewhere
in an adjacent field.

Its hours of operation are always open,
>   having no time
to do with clocks.

>   Wind carries sounds

it cannot hear

>   the way it carries

>   seeds

that will not

feed it,

the way it moves further than most

in a life that never

found

a home.

There is a quiet perfectly content without you.
The kind that says it doesn't want you around.
Get the hint, though no one says it.
Literally.

Toads splash into silence. Close down their chorale.
Buds small and bright as a pen light under
optimal conditions illuminate how far
they've come on their own.

You're not listening to a silence you
are meant to hear. The sound
of a worry still alive. Bloodroot
emerges small as a finch egg.
Shoots poke from the earth like
crayon tips from a box. Your life isn't something
they need you to share, yet here you come,
trampling the undergrowth

as Death finds your boot
a perfect fit.

THE HUNTER

In the off-season woods, not clear,
still chilly, a lone man places

a block of salt for moose to find
before hunting starts. Reserves ahead

a site for their death. To watch his prey
succumb to a taste

they will literally die for.
The gift of what he offers feeds off

all he aims to take in the end.
How time is a weapon

to load in advance.
How chance is game to be poached

if you're lucky.
How habits can be honed

to targets. How wants survive
their kill.

It moved like a hand
 forced
   down a coat sleeve.

Just the length of a man's arm.
   Punching.
Head
  the size of a small clenched fist

ready to make violence
 useful again.

Its shadow dragged behind it like prey,
  not quite dead, yet
   not quite moving.

Mink.
  Soaked.
    Wet fur
like cedar bark in the middle of a rainstorm.
Its whole body winnowed to glittering arrowheads,

  prepared for the kind of life

 I was not.

Is the one,

  surprised,

who defends its territory,

     more foolish than the one who approaches,
unasked?

    Isn't fear
the prime factor of power?

       If it's moving toward you,
it isn't in fear.

Rock face, shoreline:
its place was here.
    Wherever I wasn't.

The natural knife tip of its daggered smile.
The open mouth baring fangs of a cobra,
as if it had taken that creature in
     whole.

The mink looked for any direction,
     mine included,
     claws
   reaching down
to what is below me.

How even lives under me

     hold me up.

Snow on the branches,
but green underfoot.

The sound of a creek finally able
to pull itself out from under the ice.

Crows cry out with hungers
I keep as my own.

Even Basho couldn't escape from fleas and lice
when he lay down in the dark.

Centuries later, they're still on the page.
A flow of ink kept them alive.

An owl is a weapon laid aside
in daylight. The crows that chase it

from tree to tree are less
a black veil dragged behind than

a ripped net flung just short of its catch.
Audacity tuned to

radio silence. To an owl on a branch like a spear
off its target. Just waiting until darkness

aims it through moonlight, aligned
with a murder of crows.

HIERARCHIES, THE NORTHERN
HARRIER HAWK

In the mutual exclusion of habitat to shelter,
the harrier gives evidence enough

to decide: your final arbiter is always
above you. Small creatures – mice, voles –

keep low in grasses. Their tracks
just stop like the end

of a sentence. And a claw mark on dirt
like a signet on parchment proves

the weak do not live by their own assent.
When the hawk slowly

circles above us, it flies the way
we'd walk after dinner, taking

its time after taking a life. Held
by the appetite that holds it

aloft. Holding no part of responsibility
for whatever death is not yet its own.

A CROW'S WING (DEATH NEVER CANCELS)

Found on the path:
a crow's black wing,

severed so neatly
one half expected

a cleaver nearby,
or maybe blood,

but there was no weapon
nor explanation.

This was clarity uncluttered
by any clues.

The wing felt like the fingers
of a soft wool glove,

fluttered in a wind
only felt by its feathers

that the meadow carried
on its vast back.

How did it get here?
How did it end as

a small dark brush
sweeping the earth

up into a stillness
like an answer

giving silence a turn?
Now thought finds

itself as something heard
listening:

to the sound after breath
pulls away from the body.

The quiet that covers
a crow's severed wing

like a tarp laid over a bier.

LISTENING

Some sound, clearer than I would like it,
comes to me, speaks

what I don't want
to hear. The cry of a predator

becoming itself.
The pitch of its prey, a quick shriek

gone. The one voice
higher than the other, though

sound plays the roles
reversed.

ADDICTION, THE SPRUCE

Weeds are the first to distribute
the green that trees

still withhold in upper branches. April:
on the calendar but not

on time. Bark, root, and leaf
are reasons for each other. For each to go

its separate way. The spruce
lives fixated on only one

colour: its quills and needles
would abandon position before

they'd surrender their cache of green.
A life contained by

all that it carries. An addiction
that keeps what's alive for itself.

BLACK SPRUCE

Black spruce; strange fires
John Thompson

A black spruce toppled to
dry splintered wood is danger advancing

to better conditions. Not yet a threat
but coming soon. Fuel for the oven

it stokes in itself. The future address
of a landscape's demise

forwarded to a delivery of random kindling
stacked like junk mail, unnoticed,

unread, until air offers an invitation
of upward mobility. For tinder to rise

to the top as fire when a heat wave delivers
what waits to arrive.

The new trail was the same route to
old disappointments. Letting you lead,
I followed my sense
of what you shouldn't see
of me:
       skidding, slipping down mud,
gravel. Inept like so many times before,
confidence was a path
my life seldom followed.

Of course, I wouldn't say this.
We had reached the summit, the view
almost clear.
            The sun
looked filled as a small pail of milk.

The truth remained
too big for the moment.

FORECAST

Weather gets a new rumour
going with clouds,

clues in the cold.
Snow's white print is the news

at hand. As if there's always
something better

to be, a red-tailed hawk heads directly toward
the very same chill

that drives us back in.
So much that we missed

keeps getting ahead. Then goes even further.
We've come

to confide so little in each other we're almost
anybody now,

strangers again. Grasses tall enough
to provide their own cover

surround us as if we're
just game.

CONSIDERING THE BENIGNITY OF CLOUDS

There are clouds on the move to
the end of their edges,

close to the end of their own shapes.
Frayed where nothing was woven,

they unravel what no one wears.
Too large in size,

they're nothing to carry –
the lightness you'd feel

when you take off a jacket.
Never contained,

they'll hold a deluge above you,
what keeps your head

bowed. Compels you to look.
Without a word,

clouds direct where you're going.
And each turn shows

you went.

CHANGE

It's raining in the way that
cancels out weather,

continuing showers
that cancel out

choice. Downpours,
heavy or otherwise,

scatter. Change
has a scent that gets

soaked in the rain it
must pass through

in order to finally arrive.
Its presence is what

the rain is leaving.
And how wonderful

it is to breathe this all in.
To let your breath feel

how you love all it's given you –
till your next breath

leaves this one
behind.

MINT

Wild mint takes its lead
from its tang in the air.

Smell it. Then
look down, around,

and there it is. To be
grateful for. A fragrance fully

alive in its name.
It makes you want to lean in, lower, before it,

not exactly bowing,
but close.

RHUBARB

after Sean Borodale

Under a ragged tent-top of loosened leaves,
the rhubarb ripens,
stalks like clear hoses flushed
with diluted blood,
veins smooth as scars on healed slit wrists,
        Caucasian pink,

then a rumpled green hue deeper
      than the leaves
        that contain them.

Pull them up like arms
of drowning men. Torque
the tensions of a twisting twine.

Strip off the leaves and let them fall
like discarded bibs no longer needed
for the grown-up feast to come.

A kitchen knife slices stalks easily as bones of sparrows.

Opened raw tints seep into air,
a coating of colours
coded eons ago. An opaque thermometer
with red mercury filaments.

The tap washes through culverts that rain never reached,
douses the stalks that thrust like salmon
against a tumbling weir of torrent water.

Let them lie prone on a cutting board
as if on a creek bottom. Ready to spawn,
to lay out their flavours.

Peering into the heated pot,
a pink-hued sunset rises up
early,
       glows,
striated lines of peppermint candy cane almost sucked clean
of its striped crimson coating.

Now, pluck the pale strings.
Pull out hunger tethered to the taste
of what we let slither down our throats,
hot tongues
taking in flesh for sweetness,

       to swallow
what appetite
wants.

Don't weeds succeed each summer in reaching
from one end of a field to the other
with no one encouraging their dirt-cheap labour

though many would trample that free-range life
as, effortlessly, weeds cross over property lines,
advancing the cause for the ethical treatment

of fertilized lawns? Does the past pull
out of the way of the future, having been told
it's parked too long? Knowing the present

stalls behind it. We're always just two feet away
from the grave, one breath short
of living forever. Persistent and present

as those rail-line junkyards: scrap metal
stacked like flattened cardboard, bicycles
twisted beyond their frames,

rows of fridge doors like upright stretchers
waiting to hold some function again.
Don't they still have the integrity

of simply *being*, the act of existence
without a life? Isn't this what the future brings
upon us? All we can do is wait for the hookup,

though in whose flesh a barb lands remains
uncertain. Or by whose hand we're caught
or released. Potential cannot exist in any

past tense. Though memory does, will,
continue. Alone at night, is all you hear
the *Cries and Whispers* of a Bergman film

when the wolf is about to enter the psyche
beneath a moon the width of an axe cut?
Asleep, questions you won't say out loud

finally take their turn to speak.
Dreams of how you'd break off with lovers
against the fact

you still dream of them here.
Dreams as the weeds of your own labour.
How life takes directions

away from yourself.

ODE TO PRODUCE

At the corner, the road bends,
extends what is possible, turns onto choices

someone ignores. Red or green:
a traffic light is a product of self-inhibition

in service to others. Which some also
ignore. In supermarkets, convenience moves

to the front of the line past
misshapen carrots and tubular apples

that don't have the good taste
to look their part. There are bins full of them

at the checkout. As if what's of the earth
is not fit for this world. I'm not

buying that. Seemingly everywhere,
middle-aged men now come out in public

with close-shaved haircuts that only the young
once considered becoming. A new standard

to halt the oncoming gray. As if convention is caution
finally conceding there's a crowd safe enough

to follow behind. In the open market
for upping perfection, it's hard to admit

you are not to your taste. Opinions
hold you like lights at a corner. Ugliness

like produce you can't pitch.

GARBAGE DETAIL

I'm picking up litter left at the pond
where a west breeze

gathers paper plates like a waiter,
clearing away

what it never consumed.
There are squashed water bottles

flat as gelled insoles. Takeout food buckets
tossed and emptied, only desired

when they were untouched.
There's a ridged plastic bottle cap

you'd grip in your teeth.
No booze, no beer. Just twisted red napkins

like ripped party favours.
Wood skewers thin as infant fibulas

stripped of meat. A Chefmaster instruction booklet
alongside its canister whose

weight I'd equate to
an unlaunched torpedo. Here's

a shrivelled balloon small as a testicle.
Red plastic cups the size of child party hats

stomped in a tantrum.
The brown fecal smear of dipping sauce

wiped over cardboard cartons
stapled with ants. Poetry

is the farthest thing from my mind
as I find inspiration to collect the garbage

no one else does.
I feel sweet as icing smeared on a knife

going through memories that aren't
even mine. Bagging the litter

like evidence against me,
who's still got the time in this world

to do this. To commit
another good deed.

REPRIMAND

Whenever you say you can't stand people
perhaps you're the person

you cannot abide.
Against your nature is Nature itself:

how a meadow grows grass
for a field yet to come,

or a field secures chlorophyll's need
for more bodies. How Nature works

on an industrial scale when you consider
the cumulative count of each blade. The way

any number of grasses and stems
wait as replacements

for what they are next, without fear,
while out in the pasture, under grey clouds,

cows huddle close as bubbles on a pond.
In the scale of their universe

they're small. We're just smaller.
The phrase *strength in numbers*

is only language living on borrowed
words. The future may not have

your history in it.
The self may not hold

your interests at heart.
Maybe it's time

to be someone other than
this person who fails

who you are.

In the tree,
there's a cardinal, a male,
barely moving,

though its heart
is the flutter of a match
struck in wind.

Some of its crimson looks
dusted with powder,
as if red is the heat

burning out from its body
and grey is the ash
of its dying down,

but it won't let me near it,
no more able to accept being seen
than to stand being touched.

If I don't move, then I'm not its danger,
more a mirror reflecting
the bird's line of vision

to aim for one stem:
its avian ability to manoeuvre
through inches

with the ease of clear miles
for a perfect landing in
boughs like cut wire.

When the cardinal flies off,
I back away. When it
returns, I come in closer.

This could repeat again and again
as patience revises
its times of flight.

The two of us wanting
to see something
changed. The other

not seen to do it.

GRASSES

Grass has a winning streak with
blue stem and switchback. If the meadow

is the market, then it's flooded
by brome. Its dormancy

banks on the dividends saved
by dry stalks winnowed down

to live wire. Or some facsimile
thereof. Whittled by heat

to whatever withers.
To sting on the orders

of no one's command.
Not inhumane as much as

inhuman – the way
clover's pink bud of soft-grain rice

remains inedible to people,
preferring, instead,

to feed off the meadow. No favourites
acquire a human function

as no human cedes taste to what's
underfoot. We're amateurs

elsewhere as well as just here,
growing complacent

while grass grows against us, incubates
a field like a walk-in clinic: illness

within range but not necessarily
in sight: deer ticks, droppings,

West Nile mosquitoes.
Nature in syndication runs

old summer repeats while we lose the reception
to our own health. If we move out,

we're also moving its produce:
hantavirus. Lyme disease. Names

you can count on. For a limited time only,
good health is your own.

Some sound turns instinct on like a motor
in a squirrel that's sent running.
No danger to us. We hear sounds

that never seem newer: bird-chirp, tree-creak.
Repeat and replay. Singularity multiplied
equals a crowd. Let a leaf

be content to hang on its own, a petal be
a prettier claw. At the pond just deep enough
to indulge in some fishing, some part

of instinct nibbles at the possibility
you're already hooked by what you want
to impale, an idea that makes itself

felt in your thoughts like a snag on a line,
like cells opening tiny windows
to let in the light that's in contact

with cancer, the point where the continuum
can cancel you out. Even people who claim
no interest in nature still watch what

interests nature each day. That cyst
on your otherwise flawless back,
which never had acne but burned so easily,

may spread to seriously curtail your future
as nature adjusts what it lives with
to what it must feed,

the way a cardinal's so red it's almost
camouflaged from safety, its feathers
the form of its own fear. Is your cyst

a millimetre darker this summer,
a millimetre short of staying benign?
It seems the future can't schedule you in

at the moment, and it's the waiting
that kills you. Any second now,
you're almost there. But who said

time wants you part of its future?
As if time's just a place to provide you
with shelter once health

flees your body like a squirrel from a threat.
A day doesn't live for the hours you give it.
Or how much of you is better

than what you deserve.

QUESTIONS

Your identity is your prison
Etel Adnan

You can become good at doing things
you hate. A job, a relationship,

some position you hold while under
its power. Because you continue,

others think you care. The terms
of your contract won't permit

your departure without losing
whoever you were to that self

which others envision as the person
you are. And that self

is a place you can inhabit
for years before you imagine

a way to escape
whoever you're seen to be in a world

where no one imagines
you're different inside. If you admit to a lie,

does it mean you'll renounce it?
Lacking imagination,

do you only tell truth?
How many people sleep in a bed

with someone who wakens
little inside them, how many people

keep to a job that holds them
for hours yet holds

no commitment? What gives cowardice
such strength others serve it,

including yourself? Smiling
at people because you were told to,

knowing your place
against thinking to find one.

You see it now, don't you?
  How autumn leaves are

less than their colours.
  How grasses stitch a ripped hem

to the earth. How a wire fence
  sutures the field with a stubble

of shard-stalks rising up against one side,
  rows of streaked frost-knives

unsheathed on the other.
  How either direction confirms

that you have none, that emptiness
  wants what's alone

for itself. How you've chosen to live
  has kept you from being

less than the person you believe
  still inside you, but even you know

whoever remains
  can't rise past the damage

left in yourself, in the bottle, the bed,
  the lying bravado,

that you're wary of knowing yourself
   as you are now that years

no longer count you among their young
   once age is an inevitable

acquisition. And it's humbling, isn't it,
   to see yourself captured by

tight lines and furrows binding
   your face while your body feels like

a slack rope struggling
   to haul a dead weight

out of last night's binge,
   to find yourself up against words

like *liar* and *weakling*,
   all the more threatening

as they press at your throat?
   Now that sudden sting between the shoulders

is time prodding you closer
   toward the grave. That jab in the back

is its shovel's blade. Already,
   you hear your knees going under,

the creak of a birch tree bending in wind.
   And though you long to be more

than this person inside you
   who betrays the self you present

to the world, you know
   what he is but not how to

leave him. There's always one of your
   too many wants too personal to admit

to even yourself as your conscience
   steps away from the scene of

whatever you did to please what
   you wanted, one of those deeds

your body committed by
   whoever you were at other

moments when you wanted to see
   just how far you could go

before some part of you balked
   at going any further. Now your life

is what autumn leaves in its wake –
   snapped dry stems, yellow as beaks,

open to a sky that will not feed them.
   Twigs crack like ice breaking

beneath your boots when you've stepped
   too far away from yourself,

counting on limbs unsteady as
   crutches that sink in the mud

of October's field.
   Your breath feels the weight

of the nicotine lungs you
   drag like the wings

of a crow shot down.
   And those age spots flecked

on the back of your hands
   are dry mud spattered across

a gravestone where you kneel
   before death as if

to an altar. But why bow to anyone
   familiar enough to disappoint you

yet again one more time? Listen.
   To voice compassion

is not to feel it. You are not
   what you wanted your future to be,

just no one you want to see
   ever return.

The compulsion of snow
to keep on rising.

To descend as
tiny ripped parachutes.

To keep underfoot
what it sent undercover.

To lie shattered by
the silence it fell through when

it pulled all that
quiet down.

THE SILENCE OF SNOW

Snow is winter
dressed to be seen. Dressed
to kill.

Chilling
in the way that the source
of a shadow

is always
the light. A threat in plain sight
to blind us.

Think of how snow
masses in silence, in passive
resistance,

how snow
is the silence that swallows up sound,
though denied

a status
as something to be heard.
How it plummets

before us,
ever ahead,
a cold lover knowing

we yearn
for what spurns us.
A collie barks out of sight,

within sound.
Of snow within range:
we hear nothing.

Small talk is better
than a mute voice. A dead one.
A snowflake landing

on snow makes a sound.
If only we would listen. If only
we could.

WINTER SPARROWS

Sparrows in the spruce
stay sheltered so well, latch

onto stems that never
catch sunlight; hop through

an emptiness just barely there
to find a place that is safe for a body

to freely release
its voice.

NIGHT FEAR

Dark works its way into the house, my life.
It turns off the lamp, using my hand.

Dark leases my thoughts for several hours.
Rents out my peace of mind to panic.

It seems I'm under contract to write out my fears.
It requires no signature, only blood.

Here is the pen, a sheet of paper. Words provided
by the dark illuminate how short I fall of redemption.

My fingers grip tight around the pen,
as if fearing to let something unclench its jaws.

Anything spilled will be caught on paper.
My wrist will be the last to open.

ENTHRALLMENT (A FAN'S NOTES)

Pull meaning from life
like thorns from a finger,

leave an impression the way
a cut leaves a wound. The way grief

has a grain in any blossom.
The way a grave finds a place

when it has the right shovel.
There are hurt words on paper

you can nurse back
to death. A poem on a page

like a label on a bottle.
A scab you'd pick

to see if there's blood.
You're heading toward someone

dangerous to be,
someone who lives the life

you're afraid to. Will you ever
acknowledge how lonely you were

or continue to deny ever being
that lost? Pin your pain to a poet

to make it more personal,
let the pen be a parasite

hooked to its host.
You can always drop off

once you take what you can –
whatever you cannot take

of yourself.

BLASPHEMIES: ERASURES/EXTRACTIONS FROM JOHN THOMPSON'S *STILT JACK*

I.

Burned
on the hook,

        stone,

and fire,

can you do as you speak,

        foolish man?

II.

In this place

        too many questions

contain us

III.

I can't talk to God

        who would do my work for me.

Lord,
I'm gone.

v.

I'd rather be
dreaming
of fire

   to

      Heaven.

vi.

The moon

      in its right place lives

            in darkness

and the cold.

         Don't forget.

viii.

Behind me: words

    believing themselves.

Everything I want
will come
to give
nothing.

IX.

I get the point.
It's all in books. God knows
all the poems already.

XII.

      Looking for

              enough

   gives me

          little

XV.

Everything I want to take from the air
can look at the sun
with open eyes.

XVI.

I'm
      a story

in unspoken words,

the darkest place

to hold a pen.

XVII.

Strike anywhere.

If there's joy for one day
death cannot celebrate
the last word.

XVIII.

O my America.

Friends

dead

against

you again.

XXI.

A poem can
hook

one word or   many

      Hang on

Be quiet

Let the barb
raise the

                          ink

      to life

XXII.

I'll wait, perched,

know

        when I die

words
      run

thick with honey

XXIII.

Say it now.
I want, I want.

Back of your words
I hear my own.

XVII.

In the middle of the journey

all
find
 the
 dark.

XXIX.

The Lord giveth

            emptiness,

something
taken away.

XXXII.

For the grieving,

        God's

the final loss.

XXXIII.

Anger dies
bound to earth.

Go against the sun
to see.

XXXIV.

Grief let me climb:
I don't know to what.

XXXV.

Shame

       always destroys
what's never spoken of,

full
as always.

THE COWS OF NEW BRUNSWICK (HOMESICK)

steam / from cows dreaming in frost
John Thompson

The cows of New Brunswick
are pages to paper,

        hide under skin.

They moo to the muse, mix up metaphor
the way they mash bud and weeds
as they feed in fields that never existed,
      so right at home.

You see them plod slowly past marram grass,
rest low as a line of earthen dykes against incoming tides;
huddle like hauled boats covered in tarps,
still as the barns dotting Tantramar Marsh –

quiet creatures filling with hay.

They move as a herd of words through the mind,
nudge a bit further into places
where they canter to memory,
their eyes dark as the asphalt outside your room
      in New Brunswick,
New Jersey,

a name for a place you thought only belonged

to the home you'd return to,
a love for a lifetime.

The sound of their hooves
is leather on concrete,
                shoes on the run,

the sound of a meadow
missing its grass;

the Holstein hue of print over words
where no one,

                no one

(feel that hoof come down)

writes to say

        You're missed.

HAMMER (NOTE FOR THE BEREAVED)

At the funeral, when everyone said you were kind,
so good, they said what they wanted to

hear, not you: that goodness brings nobody back
from the grave. That your virtue spares

only those who can't deal
with your grief, who approach it like

trying to hammer a wave.
No matter how much you look out the window

to that bench where you two would sit in the sun,
there will be no one there

to prove you wrong, that someone
is more than your memory.

Truth fits your pain like glass to a window –
that clear, that sharp. Your life cut down

to one airless frame, and clarity is not comfort but
a hammer and what it can't break.

The epigraph by Louise Glück on page 1 is from "Seizure" in *Vita Nova*. Copyright © 1999 by Louise Glück. Used by permission of HarperCollins Publishers.

The epigraph by Jericho Brown on page 1 is from "Receiving Line" in *The New Testament*. Copyright © 2014 by Jericho Brown. Reprinted with the permission of the Permissions Company, LLC, on behalf of Copper Canyon Press, www.coppercanyonpress.org.

The epigraph for "Questions" is from *Surge* by Etel Adnan, Nightboat Books, 2018.

The epigraph for "Defeated (A Confession)" is from ghazal VI in *Stilt Jack* by John Thompson, House of Anansi Press Limited, 1978.

The epigraph for "Black Spruce" is from ghazal VIII in *Stilt Jack* by John Thompson, House of Anansi Press Limited, 1978.

The epigraph for "The Cows of New Brunswick (Homesick)" is from ghazal II in *Stilt Jack* by John Thompson, House of Anansi Press Limited, 1978.

"Blasphemies: Erasures/Extractions from John Thompson's *Stilt Jack*" is a series of erasure poems from *Stilt Jack* by John Thompson, House of Anansi Press Limited, 1978.

ACKNOWLEDGMENTS

Many thanks to the editors of the following publications where some of these poems previously appeared, at times in earlier versions.

Arc Poetry Magazine: "Hierarchies, The Northern Harrier Hawk"

Contemporary Verse 2: "Hammer (Note for the Bereaved)"

The Dalhousie Review: "Fishing, Tantramar Marsh"

EVENT: "Ode to Produce," "Persistence," "Rhubarb"

Grain: "Defeated (A Confession)"

Juniper: "The Trail," "Winter Sparrows"

The Malahat Review: "Blasphemies: Erasures/Extractions from John Thompson's *Stilt Jack*" (I, III, VI, VIII, IX, XV, XVII, XXIII, XXIX, XXXII)

The Nashwaak Review: "Lure," "The Silence of Snow," "Grasses," "October's Meadow"

The New Quarterly: "Windblown," "In My Jolicure Woods," "A Crow's Wing (Death Never Cancels)"

Qwerty: "Black Spruce"

Ricepaper Magazine: "Studies in Contrast"

Riddle Fence: "Change," "Red Alert"

talking about strawberries all of the time: "The Compulsion of Snow," "Welcome to the Marsh Visitor Centre!"

Tiny Seed Journal: "Considering the Benignity of Clouds"

Vallum: "Current," "Night Fear"

"The Tantramar Re-Vision," "Marsh Map Legend," and "Crossing Tantramar Marsh" were longlisted for the 2017 CBC Poetry Prize.

"Blasphemies: Erasures/Extractions from John Thompson's *Stilt Jack*" was nominated for the 2019 National Magazine Awards.

For their poetic support, thank you to Rose Scollard, David Scollard, Iain Higgins, Doyali Islam, Daniel Zingaro, and Randy Lundy. To Micheline Maylor and Neil Petrunia, for the best decisions.

Many thanks to Mark Abley, Allan Hepburn, Kathleen Fraser, and McGill-Queen's University Press for all their work and effort. Thank you to David Drummond for the beautifully conceived cover.

Deep gratitude to the enduring poetry of John Thompson. Literature creates its own landscapes.

Late as usual, this is for L.